HOME SERIES

HOME SERIES
SPACES FOR WORK

BETA-PLUS

CONTENTS

P. 4-5
A historic home with a contemporary atmosphere: the office of Catherine De Vil is furnished with a poured terrazzo floor, a forged iron window, vintage furniture and photographs by Marc Lagrange.

P. 6
The office-cum-library of an internationally renowned antique collector in a house designed by the architect Raymond Rombouts.

INTRODUCTION

T he majority of offices have a purely functional and impersonal design. Why though should we be content with a work space that is drab and uninteresting when most of us spend a large amount of time there? More and more companies are looking at the question of whether aesthetics ensure an efficient work ethic and seeking to provide their employees with a better working environment in the hope that this will improve productivity.

Another major trend is that employees are increasingly working from home, where they are able to create a space that fits their requirements and reflects their tastes. Without doubt, working in pleasant surroundings increases efficiency and creativity. What better examples of effective architecture and décor for work spaces are there than the offices designed by or belonging to interior architects and designers?

This publication showcases several beautiful offices that demonstrate that living and work spaces can be perfectly combined and that offices can be designed in such a way as to create a friendly, pleasant and personal atmosphere.

P. 8
A doctor's office. A project by the architect Xavier Donck.

P. 10-11
The office of Rik Storms, a dealer in antique building materials, with a reclaimed oak desk, timber wall panels and a floor made from reclaimed grey paving slabs.

A TIMELESS WORKSHOP

A hybrid work space that is stylish and warm, and an office that integrates perfectly with the rest of the house. This modest country house has been transformed from top to bottom and also extended to create offices and other meeting rooms for the architect Bernard De Clerck.

The house, which dates from the beginning of the nineteenth century, has been stripped of all the superfluous decorative details that have been added over the years.

The skeleton of the building – the framework and the beams – has been stripped bare and cleaned. The structure has been discreetly reinforced where necessary. The floor space has been doubled, both on the ground floor and on the first floor on the side that overlooks the garden. The garden itself has been re-designed in the style of the neighbouring authentic kitchen gardens. It opens out onto a small park, giving it greater depth and length. These spaces create an intimate and familiar atmosphere, and a pleasant environment in which the architect and his employees can work.

The skeleton of the house has been stripped bare and carefully restored.

The old front room now serves as a reception area. The addition of the fireplace accentuates the intimate and familiar character of the office. The fireplace surround is made from an old window frame dating from the seventeenth century.

The workshop extension where the architect works and meets his clients.

P. 16-17
The new workshop has large metal windows in order to make the most of the grounds to the back of the house. Carved from blocks of reclaimed natural Italian stone, the tiled floor has not been grouted.

The architect's workshop. The height of the new annex was determined by the imposing black bookcase.

The new work surface follows the line of the old master beam on which you can still see the original layers of paint. The magnificent ceiling was uncovered during the dismantling work.

P. 18
The old entrance hall of the house. The ceiling beams have been re-exposed. The new floor is made of bleached elm. The lights on the console table and the ceiling were designed by the architect Bernard De Clerck.

The landing and the work space that link the existing part of the house to the new annex. The new extension has a mansard roof in order to maximise the usable area in the roof space.

P. 20
The entrance hall with the new staircase. The small steps made of grey terra cotta tiles are new, but the design is based on an old model. The staircase leads to the employee work spaces.

The old vaulted room has been preserved. Here the wall paper has been removed to reveal the original layers of paint. The ceiling beams and cladding are also authentic. The lamp on the floor is the architect's own creation.

THE REFUGE

OF A PASSIONATE ARTIST

T he Austrian painter and sculptor Reinhold Traxl (born in 1944) studied at the Arts and Craft Highschool in Innsbruck and at the Vienna Academy of Fine Arts, where he learned the art of sculpture from Andre, Wotruba and Avramidis, and the skills of architecture from Plischke. He became acquainted with Sergei Poliakoff in Paris and undertook several important research trips to Egypt and the Algerian Sahara.

Eighteen years later, Traxl decided to make Tuscany his permanent home. He first settled in an old farmhouse and then, with the help of his friend and agent Astrid Meert, he transformed an old industrial building in Montisi into a new and highly original space where art and life merge into one. It is a stylish and highly contemporary space – a clean lined office that is extremely conducive to work.

On the wall, one of Traxl's oil on hessian works. The sculpture on the plinth (painted oak) is also the Austrian artist's own work. The lounge-chair and ottoman are by Charles & Ray Eames.

On the wall on the left, one of Traxl's PVC compositions. Above the computer, a work (oil on linen) by Prassinos that dates back to 1951. The desk chair was designed by Giandomenico Belotti as part of his Spaghetti collection.

Both Traxl's home and his workshop are housed in this modern warehouse designed by the Austrian architect Peter Thurner. Here living and working are closely intertwined.

A red Swan chair by Arne Jacobsen with one of Traxl's PVC compositions above.

The small drawer unit is by Carta and the stainless steel basin is from Agape. The matt steel tap and shower are from Axor (hansgrohe).

SPACES FOR LIVING AND WORKING

Stéphane Boens has established himself as one of the most influential and renowned character property architects. Whether it be historic buildings that evoke classic English manor houses and cottages, farm houses or rural residences, Boens gives these buildings an entirely personal touch. His career began in the United States where he spent ten or so years designing sky scrapers and was praised for his modernism.

Since 1992, Stéphane Boens has been living and working in a former forest ranger's house on the edge of a golf course. This house, which dates back to the nineteenth century, was originally very small but in around 1900 a second English-style building was added. Together they create an extremely harmonious and personal ensemble in which past and present exist side by side in the most fascinating manner. A cosy and warm atmosphere prevails throughout the house, including in the architect's office. With its elegant furniture and extensive oak parquet floor, this work space perfectly compliments the rest of the house.

In the foreground, an eighteenth century table designed by an English architect and a collection of antique mortars. The mahogany bookcase on the right of the photograph from Axel Vervoordt also dates from the eighteenth century. In the background, a black Tizio desk lamp by Artemide. The walnut floor is made of reclaimed wood.

Boens' office is the ideal working environment; it suits his lifestyle and provides an informal setting for meeting clients.

The meeting room (foreground) and the architect's drawing room (background). The oak floor is lime bleached.
The works of art are by Art & Language and Axel Hutte. The glass table with aluminium legs is by Norman Foster. Around the table are two Gustavian chairs and an eighteenth century French armchair made of walnut from Axel Vervoordt. In the back left corner is a French Louis XIII *Os de mouton* chair.

In his own office, the architect also successfully combines past and present.

Between the living and work spaces is the winter garden with a vigneron table from Axel Vervoordt, two tinted Gustavian chairs, a glass chandelier and a brick floor.

In the background, an oriental seventeenth century cabinet. The table is by Norman Foster.

SERENITY WITHOUT COLDNESS

O livier Dwek has set up his interior architecture office in an old bourgeois house that dates back to the beginning of the twentieth century.

When undertaking his comprehensive renovation of the property, he applied the same principles as you find in all of his projects, both professional and private, namely: the creation of space, an abundance of light and the use of angles and pure forms. In short, a design that is serene but not cold. This work space, with its severe and contemporary lines, maintains the same simplicity. The modern tone is reinforced by the stark black and white contrasts but tempered by the use of grand and natural materials such as wood.

The suspended corridor links the lower floor with the upper meeting room. The impressive six metre high doors underline the vertical effect that this project seeks to create. A seventeenth century Tibetan Buddha sits on the balustrade. The enormous matt-painted bookcase (6 x 6 m) is not fixed and stands away from the suspended walkway.

A landscaped office for the architecture, interior architecture and design workshop of Dwek Architects. The floor is made of poured, polished concrete. A long opening looks out onto the suspended staircase – a hypervisual element that gives the impression of space and light.

In the centre, an African ladder from the beginning of the twentieth century stands guard over the space between the floor and the façade. The first floor (landscaped office) thus also benefits from an optimal provision of light.
On the left, a *La Chaise* chair designed by Charles & Ray Eames in 1948. There is a contrast between the minimalist tone of this haven of tranquillity and the authentic elements: the original mouldings and the whitewashed brick wall.

The black forged iron table was designed by Olivier Dwek.
The brushed aluminium US navy chairs were manufactured in 1944 for the American marines and renovated by Starck.
Photograph by Caroline Notté.

A CONSTANT QUEST FOR BALANCE

T he architect Xavier Donck runs a flourishing architecture firm with around ten employees. His offices are housed in a separate wing of his own private home but he and his colleagues also work and receive clients in the private part of the house.

This interaction between the living and work spaces is essential for Donck. The intimacy of the home sharpens the mind and enables clients to discover the man behind the architect and to better gauge the way he works. Relatively speaking, the work space therefore contains few professional furnishings; the majority of the pieces are ordinary furniture that has been turned into office furniture.

Two Eames chairs. The pine floor was first sanded down and then consolidated to give it a darker colour, before finally being varnished.

The long table with oak top and painted grey legs is a family heirloom. It is often used when guests visit but it is also useful for spreading out plans and welcoming clients in an informal manner.
The large monochrome canvas is by Rudolf Stingel.

Donck has a superb view of the surrounding countryside from his hybrid private/ professional work space. The lamp dates from the 1940s.

P. 38-39
Living and working blend together in total harmony in this living room, which incorporates an enormous bookshelf full of architectural works – a daily source of inspiration for Xavier Donck. In the foreground, an Actualine settee. Lamp by Christian Liaigre.

ARTISAN PROFESSIONALISM

IN THE ATMOSPHERE OF
A *CHAMBRE DE BONNE*

F rancis Van Damme trained as a lawyer, but his eye for aesthetics and his love of authentic materials has been growing since his childhood.

Almost fifteen years ago, his dream became a reality. Along with a team of passionate craftspeople, Van Damme founded an artisan carpentry workshop making panelling, bespoke furniture pieces, bookcases and more, exclusively from reclaimed materials and antique items. The spaces he has created are therefore characterised by a very particular style.

The project presented on these pages represented a real challenge for him. He has turned an empty space (the bare and unoccupied attic of a solicitors firm) into an office-cum-library and a charming annex.

Francis Van Damme has created a work space with an authentic finish in the charming style of a *chambre de bonne* apartment.

Van Damme is passionate about his artisan carpentry work that is based on our rich rural traditions.

Francis Van Damme was able to let his imagination run wild with this project. Old panelling from Burgundy, shelves from an old textile workshop in Flanders and a bookcase made from an old village pharmacy medicine cabinet all come together to create a new and exceptional ensemble.

WARMTH, SERENITY, INTIMACY

 bumex started designing and producing kitchens in 1960.

Almost half a century later, the company has developed a solid reputation for itself as a designer and producer not only of kitchens, but also of global interior and office concepts, from the foundation work through to the finishing touches.

The simple designs are always elegant and refined. The personalised concept easily stands the test of time thanks to the advanced design. Materials that age well and acquire character over time are favoured.

Obumex has devised a collection of furniture, draperies, carpets, lighting and floors that perfectly epitomise the "selected by Obumex" concept.

Every one of Obumex's office designs gives the impression of warmth, serenity and intimacy.

The office of the managing director of Obumex, designed in collaboration with Jean de Meulder a few years before his death, epitomises a passion for pure forms.

LIVING AND WORKING

IN A FORMER *BRASSERIE*

Christine Bekaert chose to make her great passion for decorating character properties her profession.

It all started when she restored and decorated a former *brasserie* that is now her home and place of work.

She has set up her office and the exhibition room for the jewellery that she creates in the orangery next door to the former brasserie, creating a unique atmosphere for the room.

The design is classic and extremely refined thanks to the elegant furniture and old architectural features: panelling, tiled floors, etc.

This eighteenth century English door stands between large painted poplar wood panels.

An eighteenth century English
Harlequin desk.
The pine bookcase was created by
Christine Bekaert.

P. 50-51
A mahogany English regency desk (from around 1800). English and French oil
paintings from the eighteenth and nineteenth centuries.

P. 52-53
The linen curtains from Libeco and the walls in the same colour create a superb
backdrop for the jewellery that Christine Bekaert designs in Rajasthan (India).

The hi-fi system, television and other audio-visual equipment are hidden behind French oak panels.

P. 54 and opposite
The bookcase was designed by
Christine Bekaert for her client.
The *milleraies* striped rug creates
an intimate atmosphere.

TIMELESS CLASS

W hat started as her passion became her profession. Annick Colle is a professional interior designer. Her work is characterised by a sense of harmony and a keen awareness of light and space.

She is involved in the interior design of a home from the very beginning. Together with the owners, she decides on the layout of the rooms, the choice of base materials and the design for all the woodwork and her involvement continues right through to the choice of furniture and other items. All of her creations have a timeless elegance about them. Her personal preferences are evident in the combinations of antique items from foreign cultures and contemporary furniture.

This small north-facing room has been transformed into a private
office for a client. The existing oak flooring has been preserved
and treated in the same colour as the bookcase wall. Desk lamp
by Christian Liaigre.

P. 56 and opposite
Annick Colle's workshop. The floor is made of polished concrete. A
collection of materials is stored in the large cupboard inspired by a
Florentine bookcase. The heater is hidden below. The trestle tables are
made of dark stained oak.

LIVING AND WORKING ON THE DYKE

T hirteen years ago, the designers Wendy Jansen and Chris van Eldik opened their own shop in Wijk bij Duurstede in the Netherlands.

A few years later they moved to an enormous character property on the town's dyke, which is now their home as well as housing their office and showroom.

The majority of the furniture in this house has been designed by its occupants. The designers also own a wholesale business called Job Intérieur, which supplies furniture to interior design shops.

The interior design of their own home epitomises their style: an elegant, timeless space decorated in a variety of sober and discreet grey-beige tones using lime-based mineral paints from Keim.

The mezzanine is cloaked leather. The old pine floorboards are original. A matt oak table serves as a desk. In front is a black velvet bench by Julie Prisca. The halogen light above the desk is from Modular.

The landing. The original flooring has been painted. The oak table has been treated with wax. The chair (Job 01) has been re-covered with wool.

The buttoned chair with armrests (Job 08) is a personal creation. On the matt oak table are two terra cotta pots. The lamp is by Porta Romana.

Two chaises longues (Christi) covered with a Scapa rug.

In front, a buttoned foot stool. Behind, a settee by Christi. To the right, a Huygen settee with loose covers. To the left, two Huygen loveseats. The acetate curtains are by Métaphores.

This showroom is decorated in monochrome colours using grey-beige shades of lime-based paints from Keim. Wool rugs in natural colours and linen materials. The mantelpiece is made of French stone.

Job 08 chairs re-covered in black linen surround a table made of fruit tree wood.
The porcelain dinner service is by Gien.

In the foreground, a loveseat and lamp from Porta Romana. Rug from Society.

These settees were also designed by Wendy Janssen.
Curtains by Bisson Bruneel.

P. 64
The majority of the settees and chairs
are the owners' personal designs. The
carpet is by Ruckstuhl.

LOVE AND WORK

 «L ove and work: these are the secret to a long and happy life."

Francis Van Damme inherited this motto from his step father and it has determined the course of his life ever since.

Van Damme was a professional lawyer for many years before suddenly deciding to make a profession from his hobby – transforming authentic wooden items marked by the passage of time into distinctive pieces, ranging from panelling to bespoke furniture to bookcases.

In his workshop (see photographs p. 66-71) and his artisan carpentry work time appears to have stood still. Shelves from a demolished textile shop, sets of drawers from a former print works and antique carpentry tools all come together to create a personal and welcoming ensemble. For Van Damme, living and working are completely inseparable; his profession is his purpose in life.

Francis Van Damme working at the drawing table in his workshop: a passion for authenticity and craftsmanship.

The workshop looks over sumptuous countryside. The clock is a tribute to the "working people" salvaged from an old jute textile mill.

P. 68-69
Francis Van Damme literally saved the pitch pine shelves from destruction when he salvaged them from an old textile shop. The sets of draws, also made of pitch pine, are from a print works.

Francis Van Damme is not a collector but he has an immense respect for manual craftsmanship and the enthusiasm with which our ancestors used tools such as these.

P. 70
The computers are almost an anachronism in this timeless environment. An old canvas from a French carpentry workshop softens the severity of the ensemble.

P. 72-73
This distinctive cabinet was created for one of Van Damme's clients from an old records cabinet from a French administrative building. The doors and original glass remain intact.

HOME TECHNOLOGY

IN THE COUNTRY

W illiam Knoors is the managing director of the home technology systems company Bits & Bytes.

A few years ago, he moved with his wife and children from his ultramodern house to a fantastic isolated farm in the countryside. Architect Luc Dreessen was put in charge of the architecture and Gert Voorjans was given "carte blanche" with the interior design.

The result is an inspired and highly personal home, which caters for every member of the family.

This rural home has a timeless charm but is also equipped with an ingenious home technology system.

William Knoors' office at home: a place to work without being disturbed in the peace and isolation of the countryside.

P. 76-77
One of Knoors' daughters at work in the living room. The architect Dreessen and interior architect Gert Voorjans have used the available space to create a functional design that optimises contact between the family members.

This house clearly illustrates that home technology systems do not only belong in high-tech houses.

P. 78
The two-tiered room of one of the two teenagers: sleeping and working are combined on two levels.

FUNCTIONAL AESTHETICS

F or Jean De Meulder (1940-2003) interior and furniture design were in his genes. The De Meulder family were creating the most beautiful interiors as early as the end of the nineteenth century, and both his father and grandfather were celebrated interior designers and architects.

This internationally renowned interior architect opened his own studio in 1980.

De Meulder liked to receive his clients in his own environment. It was generally here that the first meetings took place and designs were created. These pages provide an insight into Jean De Meulder's work.

A solid silver Buquet lamp, originally produced in France in the 1930s and then modified by the Wiener Werkstätte.

The entrance hall. The chair was designed by Robsjohn 'Gibbings. The lotus flower vase is by the Argentinean Martial Berro and is standing on a rope plinth designed by Christian Astuguevieille.

P. 84-87
The office epitomises Jean De Meulder's vision: timeless class, natural and sober colours, simplicity, a balance of space and colours, and the integration of contemporary art.

Above left, a rope plinth by Christian Astuguevieille. The two chairs were designed by Jean De Meulder.

P. 86
A work by Christine Nicaise above a
console table designed by Jean De
Meulder.

PERFECT HARMONY

L Antique dealers Brigitte and Alain Garnier have always integrated their place of work into their daily lives: for them the two are inseparable and form a single entity. The same thought process lies behind the design of their offices. Here a classic style has been updated and refined through a subtle choice of colours and more modern finishes: the furniture has been bleached, the old armchairs have been re-covered in plain coloured linen and the walls have been painted in contrasting modern shades.

P. 90-93
The living room and work space in the first home of antique dealers Alain and Brigitte Garnier: living and working have always been well integrated here.

TRANSFORMATION OF A BARN

INTO AN OFFICE SPACE

Y oung architect Nathalie Vervenne has a penchant for old buildings steeped in history, which she respectfully restores in a simple and timeless style.

The photographs in this feature depict the restoration of a barn on an old farm, which Nathalie Vervenne converted into a friendly and modern work space from scratch.

All of the farm's original features have been lost over the years. However, by combining reclaimed construction materials that perfectly complement the rural setting (unvarnished pine and oak flooring, terra cotta flagstones, antique doors, etc.) with timeless, pure architectural forms, she was able to recreate an authentic atmosphere.

The collaboration and discussions with the client were particularly productive, which enabled her to create a highly personal working and living space.

A warm and serene working environment. The concrete floor was poured and then polished.

Pure architectural forms make for a calming, almost meditative, work space.

P. 96-99
The work space has a poured, polished concrete floor. However, in the informal and welcoming living and meeting room, the architect has opted for a reclaimed pine floor.

AN INTIMATE

AND WELCOMING ATMOSPHERE

E sther Gutmer is head of a flourishing interior architecture firm that designs interiors and entire offices and also supports renovation projects.

This feature showcases two offices designed by Esther Gutmer in a plush and sumptuous style.

P. 100-101
A business man's office in an old bourgeois house. Leather CEO desk and chairs by Poltrona Frau. The old panelling is made of oak. The cream linen settees are by Ralph Lauren, as is the desk lamp. The JNL lamps and the mahogany and glass coffee table were created by Esther Gutmer. A sisal carpet covers the floor.

P. 102-105

The library, work and reading room of a famous editor and book collector in a reconverted barn. The stained wood bookcase contains more than 3,500 works. The old oak floor has been painted mahogany. All the lamps are by Ralph Lauren, except for the lights on the bookcase that are from England. The settees around the opium table are by Ralph Lauren. The ladder is from Gallimard. The original beams have been preserved but the ladder is new. The curtains are linen.

THE REFUGE OF AN ANTIQUE

DEALER AND INTERIOR DESIGNER

A ntique dealer and interior designer Axel Pairon specialises in seventeenth, eighteenth and nineteenth century furniture, sculptures, paintings and silverware from France, England and Italy.

This feature showcases two distinctive work spaces created by the designer: the offices of a property developer and Pairon's own personal office.

Functionality plays an essential role in both designs, but in each case is counterbalanced by an intimate and warm atmosphere.

P. 106-109
These property developer's offices are designed to be practical and comfortable and also to promote a productive and relaxed working environment.
The desks are modern and simple, but beautifully complement the stained wood floors, antique bookcases, candelabra and other antique elements.
The space has a cosy atmosphere thanks to the splashes of warm colours complimented by the use of light and space.

Axel Pairon's own desk is an English Regency style partners desk from around 1820.

The built-in bookcases were designed by Pairon himself and are made from beautifully stained French oak panels from the eighteenth century.

They provide storage for some of his art books and at the same time create a sense of space in what is a relatively small room.

AN ECLECTIC VISION

H aving completed his studies at the *École des Beaux-Arts* in Lille, Jean-Marc Vynckier started his career as a window dresser, working for clothing chains and hair salons.

While spending some time in Los Angeles, he was inspired by the advent of the industrial loft conversion as an alternative and original accommodation solution.

His own home is in an industrial building and has all the characteristics of a perfect loft conversion: an abundance of space, plenty of light, sound proportions and distinctive architectural features. Vynckier's motto: "don't add anything or take anything away".

Vynckier's private office (p. 112 and 113) illustrates this vision beautifully. The following pages (114 and 115) – showing Vynckier's restoration of the eclectic and nonchalant work space of an inspired art dealer – present an entirely different approach.

P. 112-113
A contemporary and industrial atmosphere: the office of Jean-Marc Vynckier in a restored former dye works. The floor is made of poured concrete that has been stained black and then polished.

P. 114-115
The office of an art dealer in a historic building. Here the style is completely different: the armchair with its new leopard print cover standing alongside the antique desk is sheer exuberance.

A PASSION FOR PERFECTION

When establishing its new headquarters in the Netherlands, the renowned construction company Vlassak-Verhulst was looking for a representative character property that would give its offices an intimate and luxurious atmosphere, and also serve as a pied-à-terre for its founder.

The exceptional attention to detail in this lovingly restored bourgeois property demonstrates the quality that Vlassak-Verhulst is capable of producing. Only the very best designers, interior architects and tradesmen are chosen to work on the company's projects. The result is always unique and is testament to the company's passion for perfection.

This meticulous renovation was carried out entirely by Vlassak-Verhulst tradesmen.

Company employees dine with clients in this dining room complete with cupola. It is, without doubt, the most impressive room in this bourgeois property.

The private apartment for the founder of Vlassak-Verhulst. The lift leads directly to the apartment. The antique parquet floor is from a stately home.

The second meeting room.

A chaise longue on the landing. The controls for the ingenious home technology system can be seen on the table.

Functionality combined with a warm atmosphere: the perfect office environment.

TWO UNUSUAL OFFICES

C ostermans is a company that specialises in complete construction and interior design solutions for luxury properties.

In this feature, Costermans presents two offices designed for exclusive villas. The two different styles, classic and contemporary, demonstrate the breath of the company's expertise.

A classic, timeless ambiance prevails in this work space. The bookcase is tailor-made and hand painted. The desk is antique. The floor is made of reclaimed oak.

A pure and contemporary atmosphere is created by a PB Zone table from Piet Boon made from white gloss cardboard, a Bonacini desk chair and a tailor-made wall cabinet in white gloss MDF.

A PLACE FOR CREATIVITY

IN THE COUNTRY

W hen designing his contemporary home, Alexis Herbosch,
the founder of Apluz, wanted
to create a pure design in rural surroundings.

In this feature, he presents his creative
space in his home. With no comfortable
armchairs and no excessively large desk,
the almost monastic simplicity of the
design makes for a studious atmosphere.

The drawing table in the office was made by its owner from an old palette –
originally used for drying out stones – and some old oak trestles.
The pine floor creates an intimate, soothing atmosphere.

HOME SERIES

Volume 16 : SPACES FOR WORK

The reports in this book are selected from the Beta-Plus collection of home-design books: www.betaplus.com
They have been compiled in a special series by Le Figaro in French language: Ma Déco

Copyright © 2009 Beta-Plus Publishing / Le Figaro
Originally published in French language

PUBLISHER
Beta-Plus Publishing
Termuninck 3
B – 7850 Enghien
Belgium
www.betaplus.com
info@betaplus.com

TEXT
Alexandra Druesne

PHOTOGRAPHY
Jo Pauwels

DESIGN
Polydem - Nathalie Binart

TRANSLATIONS
Txt-Ibis

ISBN: 978-90-8944-047-1

Printed in China